Bringing on the Dawn

A Book of Poetry and Prose

ROBERT F. GERACE

NEWMAN SPRINGS PUBLISHING
320 Broad Street
Red Bank, NJ 07701

First originally published by Newman Springs Publishing 2024

ISBN 979-8-89061-941-9 (Paperback)
ISBN 979-8-89061-942-6 (Digital)

Contents

Light in the Darkness 

Walking down the path of broken obligations
Rolling over them like dreams nestled in a sea of despair and uncompromising conviction
Never knowing why
Only that the pain of the state of the union bleeds over the despondency of a country in disrepair.
A lone gunman fueled by hate, driven by misconception and loss, tears out the heart of the nation.
From immunity and hope to death and loathing, a dichotomy of ideologies
From bondage to freedom, from greatness to martyrdom
A country mourns for a champion of distinction and inspiration.
Courage of one's convictions changes the social order forever.
A man for history's immortality is destined to be a beacon of light in an ever-darkening world.
An eminent legacy that will stand the test of time and remind all of his everlasting vision of the world to be healed by the words of freedom and equality.

A fire burns brightly and generously brings comfort and warmth to a chilly evening.

They sit there, recounting the days and exchanging fond memories of past encounters.

The twilight grows darker as the fire grows larger, lighting the sky with a luminous glow.

The stars seem to beckon the moon to shine splendidly on a contented couple as they settle into deep conversation.

Now feeling the sensation of nightfall

Two bodies destined for converging both thought and emotion

An evening set for romance and passion

Two hearts sensing a deep affection for each other

Now as the fire grows dim, the couple huddles closer to each other.

The tenderness of each other's touch brings about burgeoning feelings of joy and fulfillment.

The fire fades into darkness as the two beloved retire to the delicate light of the bedchamber—a melding of both deep sensibilities and devotion.

The two lovers embrace each other, falling together in a conjoining of tenderness and fervor.

An evening to cherish as a beautiful memory of the star-studded night

The Journey

The road dissipates into the distance as a bright sun brings an awakening to the dawn and raises the hope of a meandering soul. The journey is long, and the road fraught with precarious encumbrances.

A soul destined for new and hopeful endeavors

He walks slowly, examining each roadblock to a profound, untrodden destiny.

The sun rises, and the road seems to open up; the distance now shrinks, and melodic strains of the cool breeze fill the air.

A respite from the pitfalls of the journey

A new direction is in the offering.

As the dawn falls away, so does the feeling of loneliness and precariousness of direction. The sun and the road seem to meld as one.

A newly discovered understanding fills a freshly opened perception of what may lie ahead. The direction now seems to have a comprehensible purpose as the sun opens the light.

So, too, does the prospect of a newly formed exuberance for life

The journey and destination now seem clear and conjoined. The journey, the destination, and the man are now one for the future.

The Rug

A worn mosaic of never forgotten thought lies unruffled on an aged carpet conspicuously nestled over a wooden floor.

Pictures of old memories stamped indelibly on a solitary mind, with each strand relieving the past in vivid color and reminiscence.

Little feet stomping carelessly on each woven fiber with dog hair still clinging to the corners

Board games with children happily playing on the soft cushion

Each patch echoing recollections of time passed

A tribute to all who have come before

A remembrance filled with hope and contentment

A reliving of poignant moments lost in time

An affection of pleasant encounters bringing joy to a wearied heart

My Heart Belongs to No One

My heart belongs to no one
Floating aimlessly on a sea of melancholy thought
Destined for the distant reaches of a concealed conscience
A slow boat without a destination continues on a rudderless journey to nowhere.
My heart belongs to no one.
And the tides beckon me to continue sailing without a port to be found.
On and on, the waves carry me as if floating to a place of unknown destination and forsaken memories.
But my heart belongs to no one.
And as the ocean continues to intensify, rolling waves bring the feeling of regret, a longing for that which was lost.
Forlorn emotions melting in a sea of hopelessness and despair
A regret of unfulfilled coalescence
My heart belongs to no one.
The days go on, and the songs die out.
You were here, and now you're gone.
The darkness comes from time to time, more often than not.
I wish you were here.
My heart belongs to no one.

A stream of yellow-white haze washes over the bright green plain like waves cleansing the refuse of a sand-covered beach.

A warm, radiant silence fills the air, and the senses with a symphony of light that only you—alone—can hear.

The heat is browning the skin to the color of its earthen womb.

You look up and smell the essence of a warm day, a day the sun brings the smell of the earth to one's nostrils and fills the pallet with the taste of happiness, summer wine, ice cream, and strawberries.

The memories of times gone by

It comes in waves, never knowing what direction it takes.
Building up tension to the point of no return
Anguish and happiness—a dichotomy of emotions
Pouncing on dreams, plodding through the day
Held captive by fits of anguish and despair
The highest high met with the lowest low.
Mania and depression—one feeling denying the other
Fighting within a haze of converging emotions, like the water rushing down the rapidly flowing creek and into a placid grotto destined for wandering thoughts.

Working to quiet the tempest and alleviate the dark musings of it being in constant torment of demanding sensations
Two voices of irreconcilable contrast
Continuing to fight the day
Capturing the ebb and flow of a mind, continuing an assault on the senses
A desperate attempt to change the direction
To feel the warm glow of the psyche slowly regaining its balance
Trampling over the compulsion and desolation
Seeing the sun again
Riding the wave to a welcoming shore
Conquering the Tiger—settling on a path to enlightenment and vanquishing the demons
A war won with intellect and the repression of despondency.
Striving to meet an ever-changing world with a newfound exuberance
Silencing the consciousness of discordant sensibilities
Awakening

The willow bends and sways in the breeze—never settling on the
  direction, unable to choose.
Destined to be directed by the caprice of nature
Languishing on unsteady roots—kneeling to the wind and rain
Forlorn in its acceptance of the fates of the forest
Unaware of its true purpose
Alone in a stand of oak

Dreams

Dreams come in every color, every shape, and every size.

To dream is to aspire.
To aspire is to grow.
To grow is to learn.

I learned that I must dream.
I must aspire.

My color is red.
My heart is fire.
My size is beyond the boundaries of time and space.

Wash away my dreams, and my fire dies.
My color turns to gray.
My size shrinks back to the limits of my body.
My time becomes the present.

I wish my dream never dies.
Without my dream, I may fall fluttering frustratingly—like Icarus trying to escape the labyrinth of this earth.

Dream to leave the labyrinth.
Soar and glide beyond the sun to the shores of your own heart.

Dream to seek out the light and let it flame up in your soul and forever shut out the night. For those who see only the night are condemned to the darkness.

If your soul is fired with the light of aspiration, the flame of growth, and the size of the goodness of the universe, your heart will remain as the winter rose that blooms in the light of every season.

Maleficent

A maleficent wind blows incessantly, bringing a portent of things to come.

Sordid dark clouds, looming ominously in the distance

The smell of fear permeates the air.

You walk on surreptitiously, knowing not where your journey lies.

Suddenly, you stop looking around for the very thing that causes the fear.

It is within—not to be understood, but only felt.

A pounding of the heart and a gripping tightness cause the stomach to wrench and grind.

You lose all thought as the anxiety slowly crawls upward, straining the throat and drying the mouth so as not to speak.

Your journey stops as you cannot see the path anymore.

Lost in a sea of confusion—wondering where it will end

Not knowing what vexes you and leaving you prey to a journey unfulfilled

Spring

The earth seems to open as new life begins its journey to fruition.

The convergence of light, soil, and water brings out the alluring beauty of new and resplendent colors destined for wonder and pleasure.

As the morning breaks, so too does the awakening of the flowers and verdant woodland gardens in their natural setting.

A comparison of two lives—nature's bloom and man's journey into adulthood

As the dew settles, it brings new life to a lush forest bound for elegance and enchantment.

The day brightens as the sun caresses the newly awakened harbingers of life renewed.

As the coach spread across the red dust trail, the small crimson peaks began to awaken and stand at attention in response to this mechanized intruder. Within minutes, we stopped as the dust settled back into the grooves made by many coaches before us. The ground begrudgingly gave into my steps as I began to climb up the jagged rocks in between the cracks and crevices of one of the enticing peaks of the gorge itself.

Climbing higher and higher in a frantic race with time and nature, I could sense the power of this land that had been taboo to all but the highest of aboriginal shamans. No one was ever allowed entry, as only the aboriginal tribes were allowed inside. As I neared the top of the gorge, the howl of the wind pierced both my senses and my soul as if to warn me of impending doom upon the possibility of my intrusion.

Reaching the top, the wind now seemed to be moaning with the haunting cries of generations of aboriginal men and the souls whose purpose was beyond my own stifled comprehension. Gazing down and out into the monolithic setting was a small enclosed plain with firm green grass surrounded by sentries of rocks guarding its very unspoiled beauty. The constant sirening of the wind continued to be a reminder of the strange sensations within and around me. I experienced numbness of both thought and expression, as if somebody was just outside me—watching me. Unknowingly, my thoughts pervaded all internalized rationalization.

I began to feel the existence of something other than my senses could perceive. I will always remember the feeling and the realization of being so small in such a vast space. A space whose only tangible recollection is the piercing in my gut, the sweat on my brow, and the feeling of insignificance. A place where reality is not of the body but of the mind. A place of power and grace carried by the wind and felt by moments of tenseness and shortness of breath.

As at Ayers Rock, the feeling of another worldly force was unde-niable. As I climbed down to the worn scarlet tracks of the coach, I would always feel that a force beyond anything I had felt before was harbored within the valley of the Olgas themselves. A force that is only understood by the aboriginal tribes. It is a place of sanctuary and ritual, a home to those who are privy to its magic.

Morning

With each starless night, there is the anticipation of the dawn.
Warmth and emerging light
One that moves the clouds
Shines down for a single moment
Enlightens a weeping flower, exalting it to open its buds and fragrant
    the air
All the while smiling incessantly at those who notice its bloom

A Vision to Behold

Stars do not align, and nightfall comes in waves, covering the light and shutting out the emotions of a punctured heart—only to be awakened by the elegance of an evening of unrivaled joy and contentment.

By candlelight, there are sounds of musical harmony, softly caressing the sensation of magical melodies. Like the beat of the heart that yields no harbor, but beautifies all who listen. A homage to the rhythmic strains of recurrent verse, as if Apollo himself brought the beauty of the muses to magnify the musical composition.

An alluring countenance of unrivaled artistry strolls down a path of unrequited love lined by lily fields bent to honor a lost soul. A soul earned by bereavement, but hearkened to life by the thoughts of a new-fashioned companionship.

Contemplation of imaginary companions playing on the willing affections of a newly unburdened heart opens to the exquisite emotion of newfound expectation. Slowly, the happiness of new and exciting thoughts pervades her very existence. Hope rains unsurpassed as a new contemplation offers a portent of sanguine things to come.

A future designed by exquisite fantasy and a longing for conviviality

To be a stalwart ship in a sea of disillusionment

Snowflake

A diminutive snowflake filters through a dusty sky, carefully bypassing the outstretched arms of a moribund oak.

The oak, seemingly reaching for the vastness of the heavens, looks beholding at the small truth this tiny white parcel apparently carries with it.

The snowflake, however, senses the quest of the oak and subtly maneuvers between its many grasps.

Oscillating, the tiny wafer floats benevolently to the frozen ground, where it is immediately drained of its existence by a single blade of grass.

The grass—immovable, somber, and desiccated—suddenly awakes with a newfound salvation of its life.

A single snowflake—so light, so unimportant, so minute, so unnoticed—is now to a single blade of grass the most beneficial factor of its existence.

One snowflake so intricately constructed, but so immaterial, has given its life to the perseverance of another.

An essence dependent upon the minute parcels of nature, the heroically beautiful but quietly intrinsic.

A Contradiction

The soft evening breezes melt into a mellow sunset as the sea rolls gently over moonstruck sands.

The sky seems to settle as inconspicuously on the shore as the morning dew settles caressingly on the beach.

The sea, the sky, the earth—wantonly display their power through a magnificent disunion of unbridled beauty and horrifying rage.

Here is the bare but complex, the spectacular but essential.

Sometimes overlooked in its nobility, but never forgotten in its wrath.

A basic beauty with the fury of a thousand demons

A rainbow and lightning—a dichotomy of existence

Grace and tyranny—the elegance of life and the deprecator of souls

So perfectly intertwined that no human cognizance can separate the common bond between the two.

Man also is a contradiction, as he suffers from the same separation, the pitfalls of affection and loathing. He is his own ruler, yet he knows not the control of his emotions. He may be beautiful but ignorant, brilliant but unpleasing to the eye.

In no way is his creation perfect, yet he is the source of dreams and the despoiler of compassion.

The worn leather moccasins, covered in dust, lay forgotten next to the deerskin jacket that hung limply beside a rusted sharps rifle.

A remembrance of days that have long passed

Forgotten memories lashed together with blood and bone

A hunter without remorse or respect

So to as far as the eye can see are mounds of flesh lying stagnant on pastures of mindless slaughter.

Before the dawn of the broken times, the plains were abundant with magnificent beasts that were

Respected

Gratified

Celebrated

Herds as far as the dawn can be seen

Staunch stock destined for food and clothing only as needed— never more

But the broken times are that of the white man

His greed

His hate

His prejudice

His lack of empathy

A hunter destined for carnage

You Can't Walk All Over Me—Song Lyrics

They say I'm a nice guy because some women think they can
walk all over me
They say I'm an easy get and I can be your pet

You can't walk all over me

I may be outward and obvious
My emotions on my sleeve
But, baby, you have to believe

You can't walk all over me

Because, baby, you see, I'm just a man who wants to be loved for
who I am, not who you want me to be
You just don't see the goodness in me

You can't walk all over me

Don't want anybody to control me
Nobody to change me
Nobody to save me

You can't walk all over me

I need to have someone to be my muse
To make me see the song lighting the sky
I never want to say goodbye

You can't walk all over me

I need to hold somebody in my arms
I need to see them in the dark
To make my heart beat to a different drum
Somebody to understand
Somebody to let go of command
Somebody to love me for what I am

You can't walk all over me
You can't walk all over me
You can't walk all over me

Old Friends

He walked slowly down the path, envisioning a day from all cares—a time to spend with friends.

While the walk is long, the anticipation keeps a keen mind open to new conversation. Something he cherishes more than any other endeavor. A challenge and a friendship are open to new ideas and new places.

Freedom from trite exchanges and small and uninteresting talk of nothing, some with nothing to say

Two friends sitting down to share their thoughts on the day, each learning from the other

Stories and facts to be shared in a well-mannered way

At first, a simple hello and a customary greeting

A hot cup of coffee and revelatory ideas from new and exciting places

Each topic brings to life a longing for knowledge and camaraderie.

Friends are hard to come by, and a meeting of the minds is a rare experience indeed.

The time wears on, and the talk dwindles as the day takes its course.

A fruitful venture that satisfies an enlightened mind ends the encounter and the long road home seems to be much shorter now.

Sometimes it happens that way.
Dreams that we make come true
Languishing in a trove of converging thoughts
Wondering if serendipity intervenes in a rush of inspired imagination
Waking moments ushering in memories of fantasy and reverie
Walking in a trance, hoping for the sun to shine in and the wind to
carry me away on waves of whimsy and exhilarating emotion
The lake beckons, and the water is enticing as dreams become reality.
Stepping on lily pads
Walking on water
Hoping to make it back to the shore

The Magical Forest

Sometimes, whimsy and dreams come together to form a story of fantasy and wonder. With that in mind, there is the large barnyard—a special place where we can only see what we believe in.

It was a typical day—blue skies, puffy clouds, a nice breeze, and of course, a rainbow.

The yard was full of all kinds of animals. Some were very common, and some were very strange! There were cows, chickens, monkeys, cats, little puppy dogs, and a great big friendly rat. There were horses, pigs, and a crazy old wild-eyed bat. An old and wise barn owl sat in the window at the top of the barn and watched over all the animals in the yard.

On the other side of the barn were the ones that were not for everybody—maybe not even for you and me. Therefore, if you didn't believe in all the things that are magical, your eyes couldn't see. There was a playful kind Griffin who had the head of an eagle and the body of a lion with wings, a watchful four-eyed fawk that had a beautiful golden body and crimson wings, a peaceful purple polka-dot pumpat that could fly, and a furry-faced ferrior who had multicolored eyes and long legs to run as fast as could be. Lastly, a big-eared, long-nosed ancient lumberat walked around all day and tried not to get fat while talking to everybody that he could.

To keep all of them protected, the large barnyard had an old weather-beaten bandy tree—a grisly barked one that talks all day. And let's not forget the catching fence—the one that moves back and forth in the air to gently catch any of the wonderful creatures before they can run away and hurt themselves. These were very special fences made of pinewood arms and moving eyes.

Then there was Lily, a sad little girl who sat on a fence watching the sky go by. You see, Lily was not special; she was just a girl. Lily was very sad and lonely, and she only had her grandpa and grandma to talk to. Her mom and her dad had left her there to go away for a year on a business trip over the ocean. Lily sighed and slumped, got up, and asked her grandpa if she could go for a walk in the forest and find out why she was so sad. Grandpa knew that it was okay because the forest was friendly and full of joy.

So Lily set off on a journey, watched closely by the four-eyed fawk. She walked into the forest, deep and magical, where flowers always grew. The light shined down the path to guide her way. So onward, she went to see what she could see. As Lily walked carefully into the forest, the flowers began to bloom and the branches began to move up and down. On and on, she walked wondering why she was so sad. What can happen to make the melancholy haze go away? Suddenly, the tree branches slowed down, and the forest became eerily silent. Lily was now feeling more afraid than sad.

Then a low rumble startled Lily as she walked on very quietly and wondered what could make such a strange noise when, all of a sudden, she heard, "Hello. Who are you?" She could not find where it came from. Again, it called out, "Who are you?" This time as she looked around, she noticed a large tree. This was a giant of a tree with a light-colored moss on some of the roots that were showing. The bark was dark and scaly with branches that looked like great big arms. This was a mighty stalwart reaching for the sky and standing by itself in a small garden of flowers and green grass. For the third time, Lily heard, "Who are you?" She was shocked as she saw that the tree had spoken. Lily could not believe that a tree could speak.

She quite meekly said, "My name is Lily. What's yours?"

The tree looked curiously as she had not seen a child in quite a long time. "My name is Okun, and I haven't talked to anybody in many, many years."

Lily asked, "How many years have you not spoken?"

"I am five hundred years old, and I have only talked to three humans in all that time."

Lily could only marvel over the fact that she was five hundred years old and only spoke to three people. Lily replied, "Don't you get lonely standing here all by yourself?"

"Yes, it does get lonely. But being a magical forest, I sometimes see my woodland friends frolicking in the grass. This makes me very happy to see all the little creatures having so much fun. Also, if I'm very quiet, every so often the fairies come out to collect food and frolic in the forest. You see, fairies are very magical as they bring happiness and joy. If you are very lucky, you may see one in the flower beds or hiding behind another tree."

Lily was now very curious and excited. "Will I see the fairies?" Lily asked.

"They are not for everybody to see. They can only be seen by those who believe in magic."

Lily pondered and said, "I want to believe, but I'm really not sure if I've ever believed in magic."

Off in the distance, the four-eyed fawk looked on, carefully listening to every word as he watched over Lily. He, too, was magic, but Lily could not see him. She was a little sad but still looking in wonderment at the tree and the flowers. The fawk, now sitting on the tree, continued to keep a watchful eye on Lily.

Okun said, "I can see the sadness on your face. What makes you so sad?"

Lily answered, "I don't know. I just feel like nobody can help me. I just don't know if I can get rid of my sadness!"

"Oh, that is sad. But maybe I can help you out. There is somebody who can help you, but you have to be careful as she can be very disagreeable if you say the wrong thing. Her name is Olivia, and she is a wise old owl who sits in a tree and looks around all day. She may help you if you can be nice and start to believe in magic. Even though you can see her, she is magical."

Lily told Okun thank-you and proceeded down the path past the flowers and the trees to a small opening by the path. There was a large tree with leaves covering all the branches. Only one branch had no leaves, and sitting on the branch was Olivia, an old owl with ruffled feathers and big blue eyes, watching carefully as Lily approached the tree. Olivia was very old and could be a little ill-spirited, so Lily knew she had to be on her best behavior. She looked around and saw the owl sitting in the tree. She was very curious as to what Olivia would say.

Suddenly, Lily heard, "Who, who, who are you? And what are you doing in my forest, little girl? You are probably in the wrong place. Go away!"

Lily tried not to be upset or cry even though her eyes welled up. Lily could only marvel at the talking owl as she said, "My name is Lily. I was hoping you could help me!"

Then Olivia told Lily, "I can see the sorrow in your eyes. What makes you sad?"

Lily very cautiously answered, "I don't know. I just feel like nobody can help me or really cares. Okun sent me because he said you can help me get rid of my sadness and believe in magic."

"Oh, I don't know about that," said the wise old owl. "That's a mighty large task. Besides, what can you give me in return?"

Lily was now confused because all she had was herself. She didn't have anything to give.

"I'm sorry, ma'am, but I don't have anything to give!"

The old owl looked down at Lily and shook her head. "Well, everybody has something to give. You just have to think."

Lily was now very bewildered as she could not figure out what the old owl meant. She looked around and scratched her head. She was stuck as she could not think.

Lily said, "I don't know what to say other than please and, if you help me, thank you."

"Well," said the owl, "at least you are very polite, and that should be good enough. Now, tell me what you want, and I'll see if I can help."

"I'm always a little sad, and I don't believe in magic even though I tried."

The old owl fluttered her beautiful white wings, flew down, and sat on the large stone next to Lily. "This is a serious problem. We will have to work on this," said the owl.

Lily asked, "But what can I do?"

"You must think, and you must start to believe!"

"How do I do that?" asked Lily.

"I said you must think. Do you have anything you can call magic?"

"No, I really don't."

"Oh yes, you do. However, you must start to believe in your heart. I will give you a hint, but you have to see the answer yourself. Now, since you came into the forest, what did you see?"

"I don't know," said Lily. "I see the trees and flowers, and I see you and Okun."

The old owl asked, "What does that tell you?"

Lily had to think and think and think. Then it came to her. "I see you and Okun, and I never realized it, but both of you must be real magic. I never saw a talking tree or an owl so wise."

The old owl just nodded and gave what one might call a smile.

Lily began to get a look of joy on her face and get very excited. "I guess I can believe even if it took an owl and a tree to show me."

Then the wise old owl's eyes opened wide and she said, "You see, my dear, nobody can make you believe and nobody can make you happy. You have to do that yourself. You are the one who can see what's magical and what makes you happy. We all have to see our own magic and believe in ourselves. If you do not believe and make your own happiness, you will never be special and you will never see the magic in everything. You can make things happen yourself, and you then will know both happiness and magic. You see the only person that can change you is you."

Just then, the fawk landed next to Lily and fluttered his wings. For some reason, Lily understood what he meant, for Lily now saw the magic and realized her own life was special.

Now it was time to go home with the four-eyed fawk leading the way.

"Goodbye, Mrs. Owl, and thank you forever." Lily felt like a new person and started skipping down the grassy lane. Finally, she came to Okun and stopped to say goodbye.

"Goodbye," said Okun, "and make sure you come back to visit."

"Thank you for everything, Mrs. Okun, and I will always come by."

Happily, Lily skipped out of the forest and walked down to the farm. Just as she came to the fence, she stopped in amazement; and for the first time, she saw all the special and magical creatures behind and on the fence. There was the playful griffin, a purple punpat, a fuzzy-faced ferrior, and an old lumberat. Lily finally could smile and be happy, for she became special by taking care of herself. She realized that to be special and to be happy, you must help yourself, for only you can make yourself change.

In the distance, the old farmer glanced and saw the look of wonder on Lily's face. He, knowingly, just smiled.

Setting Sun

It succumbs slowly to the night, falling endlessly in a kaleidoscope of light.

Converging waves shooting in all directions, parsing the sky with slivers of color, fading as night falls

With each falling shard, a globe beckons bygone days and begins to wash the sky with a natural luminescence.

A sharing from one exquisite sphere to another

A waking of the night, as the dwindling of the day fades into the now brightened evening

The last breath of a dazzling day

Memories lost in the dissolving of the light as a brilliant globe kisses the moon good night.

A Tree Grows in the Sidewalk—a True Story

There was a little sapling growing on the sidewalk in New York City, searching for the sun as it wished for others to join its lonely existence.

Wanting for water, waiting for the touch of forest worn hands, it sits quietly contemplating the future, hoping for nourishment.

A young couple walks by—stopping to see this new addition destined to brighten the bleak day.

The couple decides to tell each other how this stately tree came to be. First, he said, "You make a hole, then you put the dirt back in, and then you plant the tree."

See, it's easy; they both agree; that's the way it should be.

Happy they both have solved the planting of the tree, they begin to walk away.

Little did they know that's not the way to plant the tree as the tree knew better than thee.

They relished in their foolishness and happily wandered away, thinking they had solved the problem of the tree.

Not knowing there was no problem with the tree, it was there to see and be just a tree.

Raising to the sky, hoping to see the sun again, to make the tree so beautiful to see

Breeze

The morning breeze breaks the waves on a placid ocean, destined to sweep me away to a pleasant memory yet realized.

Only to be wandering on a ship without oars
Waiting for the tide to wash over me and carry a lost soul over land and sea

Driven to land, riding on Poseidon's graces to that place where dreams are real, and love lost is met with open arms

Waiting for flowers on the water

A delicate white rose lays longingly on the silk pillow of dreams, waiting for affection and pining for the return of castaway passion.

The petals stay bright with the hope of a new joining in a lasting convergence of enlightened affections and alluring adoration.

As your imagination and sensibilities slowly unburden, you can see the dawn and the emergence of newly opened desire.

The shimmering petals stay vivid and beguiling, now seeing a hope renewed.

An awakening of a shining moment as if walking on clouds of rapture

A recollection of lost passion and a burgeoning enchantment of two hearts beating as one

The rose slowly curls and softly sways its petals as to bow to a love remembered and a destiny to be fulfilled.

Bringing Out the Light

She walks in the shadows, bringing out the light.

A vision of beauty and enchantment as if touched by the hand of Aphrodite herself

She garners looks of desire and exhilaration as she saunters through the gazing eyes of wishful seduction and enchanting allurement.

An enchantress reminiscent of the sirens of old

Nature acquiesces to a figure of mystifying countenance and a portrait of untold elegance.

The forest seems to surrender to her presence as the sun casts a beam of luminescence over a now well-lit path.

A glow emanates from an aura that surrounds her.

The wind kisses her cheeks and turns them to an angelic red hue as if a rose caressed her skin.

She walks on, bringing joy and excitement to all who wander past.

An alluring figure for all to see, destined to fulfill dreams and enlighten the day.

The sea pounds endlessly against weather-torn rocks destined for becoming nature's antiquities.

Beaten by years of regret pounded over and over against the same tide

A conversion of nature and reasoning

Years and years of the ebb and flow rolling in and out like the feelings of a soul searching for contentment and compassion

A soul lost in a torrent of conflicting emotion and contemplation

The ocean continues to pound the shore as the sand and rocks bow respectfully to the power of the sea.

From tranquility to a sea of dissolving excitation

A journey through waves of contempt and loneliness only to roll back against the shore of weatherworn, unrequited love.

To continue on against the tide of despair and into a new awakening of an enticing dawn

To fight against the night

Delirium

On the verge of madness
Walking aimlessly, ambling back and forth without purpose,
over the well-worn floor
Stunted by jumbled thoughts—senseless in their meanderings
The TV blaring—not understanding the words
Drunk with fear—not knowing what the future holds
Talking to one's self—arguing, losing the confrontation, disconcerting in its anger
Adrift in the sea of confusion and agitation, destined to falter in misconstrued celebration.
Longing for peace, tormented by the loss of lucidity
Yelling in the night, not knowing why, crippled by anxiety, unable to terminate the pain!
Torn apart by the conjuring of past reprisals
Unsatisfied by the lack of coherent cognition
Falling deeper into the abyss, not knowing what the future holds
Languishing in distorted reasoning, burdened by the contemplation of impending delusions
Holding back the screams and wiping away the tears
Afraid of the dark, avoiding the light
Distressed by the realization of the threat of imminent madness
Alone in a world of discontent
Petrified—never realizing happiness
Tortured

Sand

The cool evening breezes caress the starry sky as a ray of moon-light filters through the glittering heavens, resting itself slowly on the golden sands.

A small wave breaks over the shore, and at the same moment, more luminous shards of light bring into view the glittering clash of sea and sand.

The shore, now shining as if touched by some immortal hand, seethes with a new shimmering life; a life given to it by the greatest and most abundant of all the physical worlds graces.

Here, something seemingly so lifeless, so immaterial, has found love, a love through its very touch has made it glow and rock with senseless abandon.

How can a minute particle of sand express, with no human emotion, the feeling it has received by the touch of one of nature's most powerful yet caressing forces?

A touch that for no apparent reason has brought a beautiful glory to a nonliving bit of sand.

Silence

Listen to the **child**
Listen to the I can't
Listen to the I won't
Listen to the have-nots
Listen to the loneliness in the corner of the room
Listen to the impossible

Speak to the **child**
Speak to the I can
Speak to the I will
Speak to the will have
Speak loudly to resonate off the walls
Speak to pull in the corners of the room
Speak only to the possible

Then listen closely to me
Anything can happen **child**
Anything can be

They glide from pedal to pedal on gossamer wings with tiny leaf hats and pointy shoes all shimmering in the evening light.

Little flyers surrounded by fireflies lighting the way to an evening's delight

The wee sprites begin their evening's wizardry, fluttering down to the verdant forest floor as if hummingbirds filled the air.

Busy bees scurrying back and forth, teaching green wings how to fly, gathering food, granting wishes, and detecting bad dreams; and as the urchin's curiosity could not be quenched, they change bad dreams to pleasant.

They only come unbeknownst by any human sight.

From leaf to flower

From soil to tree

From woodland imps to invisible phantoms

The diminutive pixies, with darkness turning to light, fly away on translucent wings, leaving no trace of the night's enchantment.

They bring joy and hours of kindness, love, contentment, and a convergence of beauty, empathy, and concern.

A harbinger of things to come, destined for new and exciting adventures.

The Letter—Song Lyrics

I'm a letter your heart never received
A poem you never read
An envelope you never opened
A line you never read and words you never said
Because you didn't care—it seems you never did
You broke a heart filled with promise and joy
You left without a word, never saying goodbye
Baby, you never knew what you lost
I tried to tell you, but you wouldn't listen
You never saw inside me
You never cared to know
You missed the joy you would've had
But, baby, you're just a stamp on somebody else's letter

Nothing

A blank sky folding into an endless night
Floating in the vacuum of an empty space
Devoid of stars
Lacking emotion
Without love

Fighting within oneself to conquer the scourge
Losing the courage to fight on

Wallowing in the loneliness of an empty existence
Never to be touched by the light of a warm heart
Never to hear a loving word

He never meant to fall, embracing a longing for beauty that belies and intersects his solitary thoughts.

A craving for acceptance and togetherness

Finding an intimacy between them

Soft melodies that sing of harbors yet to be docked

Sadness and sorrow, grief-stricken for the loss from a bite of despair

A bold reason for the descent

A longing for her touch

A wanting of the heart

A music from within a forlorn mind

A destiny yet to be found

And the journey begins.

A long path through woods and streams, through deserts and fire and ice—a road to desire and hope

On and on, the trek continues down and down through hate and hopelessness.

To lost love

Through suffering and remorse

Finally, into the furnace, longing for reunion, yearning for affection

Who stands between love and despair? A force that condemns a life spent on wicked endeavors

An anger, a hate, a sadistic punishment for all who have digressed

But the lyre plays and enticing strains touch the soul with beauty and delectation.

A sound so alluring as to cut the air with warmth and anticipation of love reimagined

A song that melts a frozen heart and changes one's musing forever

He who reigns supreme over the land of misery and pain is smitten by the music of love.

So too comes the reckoning
The chance for a conjoining of two hearts meant for a future of
deep affection and contentment
The long walk to peace and intimacy
A love that must follow one another to be inseparable forever
But there is the decree. Do not look back to see if your love
follows.
Keeping the passion in your heart
Only to come to the end of their journey and look back on your
longing and contentment
To break the rules and lose love forever
For faith has left you and condemned your bride to loneliness
and anguish.
Two hearts that suffer from love unfulfilled
Only to sing a lonely song and play the music for all the souls
to hear
Abandoned and searching
A song lost in a sea of disillusionment

A Winter's Scene

The branches covered in snow bend slowly, genuflecting to the ground, giving praise to winter's frigid preeminence.

Beauty and heartbreak all in the same scene

A cacophony of nature's forces

A whiteness of peace and tranquility, lost in an onslaught of energy

The convergence of power and grace destined to conquer and beautify

All in the same time

All in the same place

All in the same color

All in the same emotion

A blanket of warm thought and frozen perception

A dichotomy of life and death succumbing to uncontrollable forces destined to decide life's journey

The old black man, tattered and tired, walks on a bed of broken promises—sharp and still jagged.

Never worn down by time, as if time itself stands still

The winds have not changed, and the breezes go cold, relentless, and without empathy, as the years are destined to repeat themselves on streams of anger and hate.

Stoked by the fire of loathing and misunderstanding

Seeded by decades of denying the freedom of the land

Lost in a sea of contempt and subjugation

Generations repeat themselves as if the years never changed

And the winds continue to escalate and drive the destinies of all society in directions of animosity.

The rain comes and brings with it a malevolence that continues to cripple an already broken land.

So goes the raging storms of all mankind, an agony with no antidote in sight.

A dark foreboding of things that have passed and those yet to come

Senses

I write, but I can't read between the lines.
The sorrow of the pen scratches resoundingly against the paper.

I see, yet I am blind.
Blind by the loss of my happiness
Blind by losing sight of my soul

I hear, yet I do not listen.
The white noise pushes out thoughts from the wail of pain.

I feel, yet I am numb.
Your touch is but the cold fingers of life, freezing my ambition and
hardening my emotions against the iciness of a forlorn heart.

I hope, but I lose thoughts of a pleasant recollection.
Thoughts that are lost in a myriad of crumbled expectations

The tracks run straight and true as they fade into the distance, rusted steel weatherworn by years of disrepair.

The rails are overgrown with the gnarled jungle of weeds and stubble, wanting for life.

Forgotten memories that have become lost in a dark foreboding of bygone days

A forlorn picture of corroded thoughts that have lapsed into oblivion

Not a conductor in sight

No whistle, no sound of an engine's roar

The railroad cars have dissipated into a white cloud of lost destinations.

It wasn't always this way, not dark and misgiving, but bright and shiny.

Rails that glistened in the light.

Cars packed with cheerful passengers leaving for depots to answer life's mysteries

A journey to stations of new and encouraging expeditions—lives moving on to places of enlightenment and hope

Excursions to quarters of contentment

New adventures intended for eminence

Hope for a new life, a future of impending erudition

The start of burgeoning days filled with tranquility and astonishment

A life transformed by a journey into the future

And the whistle blows signifying a stop to new memories of days that will pass.

Wandering Soul

She walks in a diaphanous ivory gown shimmering in the sunlight, strolling down a path of carefully manicured grass lined by roses, spreading their scents to all who wander by.

A vivid picture of the beauty of life, a joy to see and behold

As she continues, the very flowers seem to bow to her presence.

An alluring figure, a portrait of an artist's rendering of longing and love, destined to warm the heart of an embittered conscience.

As she saunters down the luminous path, the sun beckons and casts a perfect painting against the morning's light. A shadow emerges, reflecting a wish for a promise of gaiety and bliss.

Long strands of flaxen hair glistening in the radiance of the rising sun accentuate the angelic vision of love reimagined and hope for a future of contentment.

On and on she wanders deeper into the garden of delights, hoping for enchantment and devotion to be fulfilled.

She ponders on the day, looking for a sign to recapture all her affection and yearning from a soul lost in thought, waiting for passion to come.

She notices a single ray of light, warm and vibrant, caressing a single blossom blooming in a pool of tranquility.

A sign to awaken an embattled soul and a tribute to a reemergence of long-lost emotion

A single flower brings a remembrance of heartfelt joy and the desire for unique and new intoxicating ports of call.

The day brightens, and the feeling of despair seems to melt in the sunlight.

A slow emergence of beauty awakens the long-lost ecstasy of forgotten happiness as a tormented heart heals in the morning convergence of brilliant light and a newfound exhilaration.

I told you once, and you didn't listen.
I told you twice, and you didn't hear.
When the time is fast and the feeling short, I said

Honey, you're not done yet
Oh, darling, you're not done yet
You're not done yet

I see that look in your eyes, that feeling of desire—the hearts that beat on fire—faster and faster as it puts a smile on your face.

Oh, baby, baby, you're not done yet
You're not done yet

I want to feel your arms around me with your hands sliding back and forth, and I want to see your face looking as if to say I love you
But words don't come, and you falter, looking back as I try to tell you

Baby, you're not done yet
Baby, you're not done yet

Looking for eyes that don't wander and hearts that come to one
I know you're going and I won't see you again

But you're not done yet
You're not done yet

Because, baby, baby, you need to know where the big hand and
the little hand meet
But you don't understand

You're not done yet
You're not done yet

Acknowledgment

I would like to thank Linda Klimek for her invaluable help in editing the manuscript.

Robert F. Gerace has spent thirty-eight years as an educator, coach, writer, and theater director. He served as past president of the New York State Theater Education Association and a former member of the New York State Department of Education's Advisory Council on Integrating the Arts into Education. Mr. Gerace is an honorary life member of the New York State Congress of Parents and Teachers. Early in his career, he was active in politics as the Monroe County media director for a United States senatorial candidate. He is an avid writer as well as a sports, theater, and dance enthusiast. His first book, *Chasing Away Sunsets*, can be purchased on Amazon. He is retired and lives in upstate New York.

9 798890 619419